FOOTBALL TRIVIA

By Tyler Mason

SportsZone

An Imprint of Abdo Publishing
abdopublishing.com

abdopublishing.com

Published by Abdo Publishing, a division of ABDO, PO Box 398166, Minneapolis, Minnesota 55439. Copyright © 2016 by Abdo Consulting Group, Inc. International copyrights reserved in all countries. No part of this book may be reproduced in any form without written permission from the publisher. SportsZone™ is a trademark and logo of Abdo Publishing.

Printed in the United States of America, North Mankato, Minnesota
082015
012016

Cover Photo: Jeff Haynes/Panini/AP Images
Interior Photos: Jeff Haynes/Panini/AP Images, 1, 4; AP Images, 7; Tony Gutierrez/AP Images, 9; iStockphoto, 11, 21; Darron Cummings/AP Images, 12; Tom Olmscheid/AP Images, 14; David Stluka/AP Images, 17; Roland Weihrauch/Picture-Alliance/DPA/AP Images, 19; Bill Haber/ AP Images, 22; Jack Smith/AP Images, 25; Sal Veder/AP Images, 27; Jack Dempsey/AP Images, 29; Arthur Anderson/AP Images, 31; Dave Einsel/AP Images, 32; Vernon J. Biever/AP Images, 35; Pro Football Hall of Fame/AP Images, 37; Marco Ugargte/AP Images, 39; AJ Mast/AP Images, 41; Chris O'Meara/AP Images, 42

Editor: Patrick Donnelly
Series Designer: Jake Nordby

Library of Congress Control Number: 2015945765

Cataloging-in-Publication Data
Mason, Tyler.
 Football trivia / Tyler Mason.
   p. cm. -- (Sports trivia)
 ISBN 978-1-68078-003-1 (lib. bdg.)
 Includes bibliographical references and index.
 1. Football--Miscellanea--Juvenile literature.   2. Sports--Miscellanea-- Juvenile literature.   I. Title.
 796.332--dc23
                                                              2015945765

CONTENTS

It is hard to argue that any sport is more popular in the United States than football. The National Football League (NFL) began play in 1920. Today it is the most-watched league in the country. Many great players have played in the NFL. They have set and broken many amazing records, too. This book examines the greats of the game and the records they hold. It also looks at some fun facts and stories from the history of the NFL. Do you think you know football? Read on to find out!

*All statistics and answers are current through the 2014 NFL season.

CHAPTER 1

ROOKIE

Q **Which is the only team to finish an NFL season undefeated?**

A The Miami Dolphins were a perfect 17–0 in 1972. Miami defeated the Washington Redskins 14–7 in the Super Bowl to clinch its perfect season. No team has gone undefeated since then. The New England Patriots came close in 2007. They won all 16 regular-season games and two playoff games. But they lost to the New York Giants in the Super Bowl to finish 18–1.

Q **Which team won the first Super Bowl?**

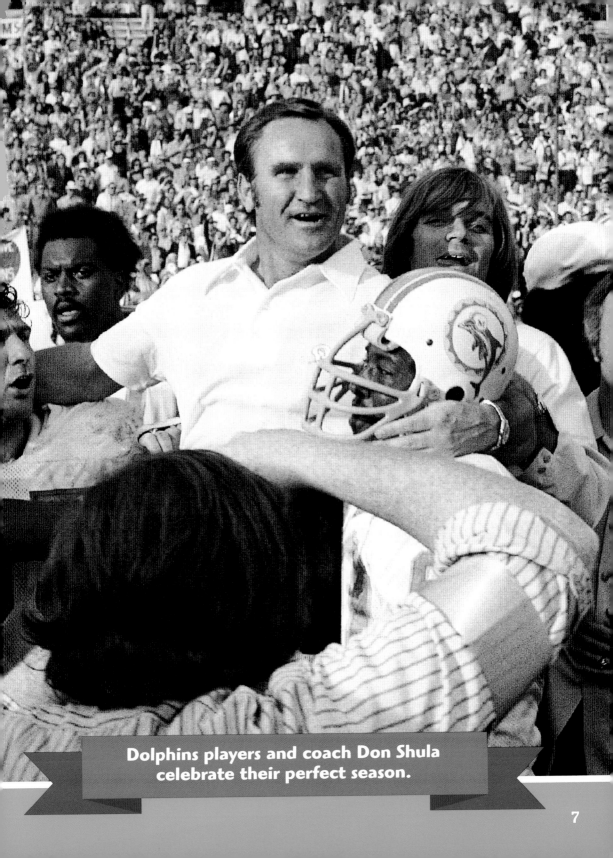

Dolphins players and coach Don Shula celebrate their perfect season.

A The Green Bay Packers defeated the American Football League (AFL) champion Kansas City Chiefs in the first Super Bowl. The game was played on January 15, 1967, in Los Angeles. Quarterback Bart Starr led the Packers. He threw for 250 yards and two touchdowns. Green Bay also won Super Bowl II the next year.

Q Which team has won the most Super Bowls?

A The Pittsburgh Steelers won their first Super Bowl after the 1974 season. They won three more in the 1970s and again after the 2005 and 2008 seasons for a total of six Super Bowl victories. Pittsburgh has played in eight total Super Bowls.

Q Which quarterback has thrown for the most touchdowns in NFL history?

A Peyton Manning has thrown a record 530 touchdown passes. Brett Favre previously held the record with 508. Manning set the record on October 19, 2014. He connected with Denver Broncos teammate Demaryius Thomas for the record-setting score.

Q Which running back holds the record for the most career rushing yards?

A Emmitt Smith finished his career with 18,355 rushing yards. Former Chicago Bears running back Walter Payton previously held the record. Smith unseated

Payton on October 27, 2002. Smith's record-breaking run for the Dallas Cowboys came on an 11-yard gain against the Seattle Seahawks.

Q **Which two teams play every year on Thanksgiving Day?**

A Games in Detroit and Dallas are a big part of the Thanksgiving football tradition. The Detroit Lions faced the Chicago Bears in their first Thanksgiving game in 1934. The Cowboys played their first Thanksgiving game in 1966. They hosted the Cleveland Browns. Detroit is 35–38–2 on Thanksgiving. Dallas has a record of 29–17–1 in Thanksgiving games.

Q **Where is the Pro Football Hall of Fame?**

A Its home is Canton, Ohio. That city is also where the NFL was founded. The Hall of Fame opened in 1963. It has expanded many times. A 46-person committee chooses which players are inducted into the hall every year.

The Pro Football Hall of Fame opened its doors in 1963 in Canton, Ohio.

Q Which quarterback has thrown the most career interceptions?

A Brett Favre holds that record and many others. After all, Favre started more games (298) than any other NFL player. Favre threw for the most career yards (71,838)

Peyton Manning was a four-time NFL MVP with the Colts.

in NFL history. He briefly held the record for the most career touchdown passes (508). But Favre has also thrown the most interceptions with 336. That is 59 more than George Blanda, who is second. Favre set the record in 2007. Washington Redskins safety Sean Taylor intercepted one of his passes to set the record.

Q Which team has the most victories in NFL history?

A The Chicago Bears have been a team since the 1920s. So it makes sense that the Bears' 752 wins are the most of any team in the league. Seventeen of those wins have come in the playoffs. But just one of the

WHICH PLAYER HAS WON THE MOST MOST VALUABLE PLAYER (MVP) AWARDS?

Peyton Manning has been named NFL MVP a record five times. Four of those awards came when Manning was with the Indianapolis Colts. Manning's fifth MVP came in 2013 with the Denver Broncos. Legendary Cleveland Browns running back Jim Brown and longtime Green Bay Packers quarterback Brett Favre both won the MVP Award three times.

752 wins was in the Super Bowl. Chicago's only Super Bowl victory came after the 1985 season. However, the Bears won eight championships before the Super Bowl began in the 1966 season.

Q Who holds the NFL record for the most rushing yards in a game?

A Vikings running back Adrian Peterson ran for 296 yards against the San Diego Chargers on November 4, 2007. Baltimore Ravens running back Jamal Lewis had the old record of 295 yards. Peterson carried the ball 30 times against the Chargers. His longest run that game went for 64 yards.

Q The Super Bowl trophy is named for which former Green Bay Packers coach?

A Vince Lombardi led the Packers to five NFL titles in the 1960s. The last two championships came in the first two Super Bowls. Lombardi died in 1970. Four months later, the NFL named the Super Bowl trophy after him. Lombardi finished his coaching career with an overall record of 105–35–6.

CHAPTER 2

VETERAN

What do fans call the Green Bay Packers' famous touchdown celebration?

A The name of the celebration is the Lambeau Leap. It comes from the name of the Packers' stadium, Lambeau Field. Green Bay safety LeRoy Butler did the first Lambeau Leap after a big play in 1993. Defensive end Reggie White recovered an Oakland Raiders fumble. Then he flipped the ball to Butler, who ran into the end zone. Butler jumped into the stands and was mobbed by Packers fans. Players have been doing it ever since.

Packers running back John Kuhn performs
the Lambeau Leap in 2010.

A Patriots quarterback Tom Brady holds both of these records. He has thrown for 7,345 yards in the playoffs. Brady also has a record 53 postseason touchdown passes. Brady has played in 29 career playoff games.

Q On which continent did the NFL start another league that ended in 2007?

A The NFL started a league in Europe in 1991. The name of the league changed several times. It was first called the World League of American Football. The name then changed to World League, and then to NFL Europe. It was called NFL Europa in its final year.

Q Who holds the NFL record for the most consecutive games started?

A Brett Favre started in 297 straight games to set a new record. His streak started in 1992 with the Packers. It lasted until 2010, when he was with the Minnesota

Vikings. Favre broke the record of longtime Vikings defensive end Jim Marshall. Marshall started 270 straight games from 1961 to 1979.

Q Who holds the record for the most quarterback sacks in a season?

A Sacks did not become an official stat until 1982. Since then, no player has had more sacks in one season than Michael Strahan. The New York Giants defensive end had 22.5 sacks in 2001. Kansas City's Justin Houston almost broke Strahan's record in 2014. Houston finished the year with 22 sacks.

Q Which stadium has hosted the most Super Bowls?

A The Louisiana Superdome in New Orleans has hosted the Super Bowl seven times. The first Super Bowl there was in 1978 when the Cowboys beat the Broncos. The most recent Super Bowl in New Orleans was in 2013 between the Baltimore Ravens and San Francisco 49ers. New Orleans hosted three other Super Bowls at Tulane Stadium before the Superdome was built.

Q Which player is the all-time scoring leader in NFL history?

A That record belongs to a kicker. Morten Andersen finished his career with 2,544 points. He was a kicker for 25 seasons in the NFL. Andersen played for the Saints, Falcons, Giants, Chiefs, and Vikings.

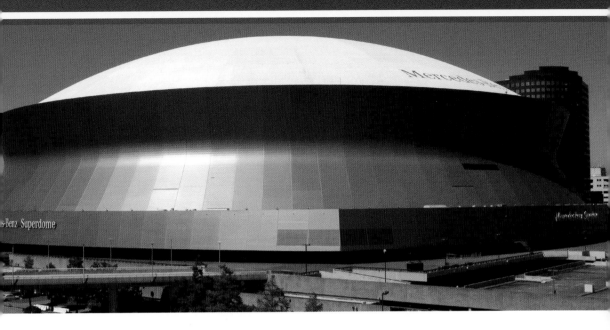

The Superdome has seen its share of Super Bowl games.

Benz Superdome

Q Which is the only team to appear in four straight Super Bowls?

A The Buffalo Bills reached the Super Bowl four seasons in a row. Their first came after the 1990 season. Unfortunately for the Bills, they lost all four.

Q Which league merged with the NFL in 1966?

A The AFL began play in 1960 as a competitor to the NFL. The two leagues began merging in 1966. They played separate regular-season schedules through 1969.

Each year the two league champions met in the Super Bowl. In 1970 the NFL broke into two conferences. The NFL's Cleveland Browns, Pittsburgh Steelers, and Baltimore Colts joined the 10 AFL teams to form the American Football Conference (AFC). The remaining 13 NFL teams became the National Football Conference (NFC). The conferences hold separate playoffs. The two conference champions then meet in the Super Bowl.

Q How many head coaches have won four Super Bowls?

A Two head coaches have won the Super Bowl four times. Chuck Noll won four with the Pittsburgh Steelers in the 1970s. Bill Belichick won his fourth Super Bowl with the New England Patriots in February 2015.

Q When was the NFL formed?

A The American Professional Football Association was founded in 1920. In 1922 the name was changed to the National Football League.

WHICH PLAYER HOLDS THE RECORD FOR THE MOST CAREER POINTS BY A NON-KICKER?

Wide receiver Jerry Rice scored more points than anybody other than kickers. He finished his career with 1,256 points. That ranks 32nd all time in NFL history. Rice caught 197 touchdown passes and rushed for 10 touchdowns. He also recovered a fumble for another score and caught four two-point conversions.

CHAPTER 3

CHAMPiON

Q San Diego's LaDainian Tomlinson set the single-season touchdown record in 2006 with 31. Whose record did he beat?

A Tomlinson broke Seattle running back Shaun Alexander's record in 2006. Alexander had scored 28 touchdowns one year earlier. Tomlinson's record-breaking run came in a three-touchdown game against Denver.

Q Which team scored the most points in an NFL game?

A Washington scored 72 points on November 27, 1966, to beat the New York Giants. The final score of the game

LaDainian Tomlinson rumbles in for one of his 31 touchdowns in 2006.

was 72–41. Sixteen touchdowns were scored in that game. Washington scored 10 of them.

Q Which two colleges have produced the most Pro Football Hall of Fame players?

A Both Notre Dame and Southern California (USC) have sent 12 former players to the Hall of Fame. Joe Montana, Jerome Bettis, and Tim Brown are among the Notre Dame inductees. Hall of Famers from USC include Marcus Allen, Lynn Swann, and Junior Seau.

Q George Blanda played longer than anybody in pro football history. How long did he play?

A Blanda spent 26 seasons in the NFL and AFL as a quarterback and kicker. He began his career in 1949 with the Chicago Bears. Blanda retired with the Oakland Raiders after the 1975 season at age 48. During his career, he threw 236 touchdown passes and made 335 field goals.

Q Which team has more than 81,000 names on its waiting list for season tickets?

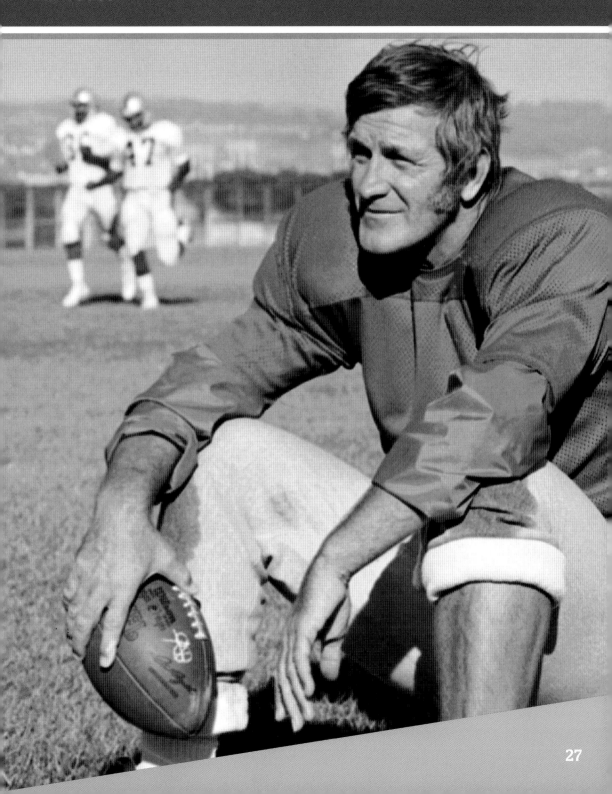

A It takes a long time to get season tickets for the Green Bay Packers. Some fans wait at least 30 years to get their tickets. Green Bay's season tickets have been sold out since 1960.

Q Hall of Fame fullback Ernie Nevers holds the record for the most points scored in a game by one player. How many did he score?

A Nevers scored 40 points for the Chicago Cardinals in a game in 1929. He ran for six touchdowns and kicked four extra points. Chicago won the game 40–6 over the Chicago Bears.

Q Which Vikings player picked up a fumble and ran 66 yards to the wrong end zone for a safety?

A Defensive end Jim Marshall did that in a game at San Francisco in 1964. He made it all the way to the end zone without realizing his mistake. Marshall and the Vikings still won the game 27–22.

Matt Prater follows through on his record-setting 64-yard field goal in 2013.

A Matt Prater kicked a 64-yard field goal for the Denver Broncos in 2013. Four kickers had previously made a 63-yard field goal. Prater's record-setting kick happened in Denver. So did two of the 63-yarders. The ball tends to carry farther in Denver's thin mountain air.

Q Which two players combined for the "Immaculate Reception" in the 1972 playoffs?

A Steelers quarterback Terry Bradshaw threw the ball. Running back Franco Harris caught it—eventually. Bradshaw's pass to John Fuqua was deflected near midfield. Harris scooped up the ball just before it hit the ground. He ran to the end zone for a 60-yard touchdown. Harris scored with just five seconds left in the game to give Pittsburgh a 13–7 win over Oakland.

Q Which NFL team began by losing its first 26 games?

A The Tampa Bay Buccaneers got off to a rough start. They joined the NFL in 1976. The Bucs went 0–14 that year. Then they lost their first 12 games in 1977. Tampa Bay finally broke through with a 33–14 win at New Orleans on December 11, 1977. The Bucs also won their next game.

Q The Buffalo Bills made the biggest comeback in NFL history against the Houston Oilers. What was their largest deficit?

A The Bills trailed the Oilers 35–3 in the second half of an AFC playoff game on January 3, 1993. Then backup quarterback Frank Reich led them to 35 straight points. Reich threw three touchdown passes in seven minutes during the comeback. The Oilers kicked a field goal to tie

Rob Bironas celebrates with holder Craig Hentrich after Bironas's eighth field goal of the day beat Houston in 2007.

the score, but Buffalo won the game in overtime 41–38.

Q Which two San Francisco 49ers combined for "The Catch" in 1982?

A Quarterback Joe Montana was on the throwing end of the play. Wide receiver Dwight Clark caught the pass. The 49ers trailed the Cowboys in the NFC Championship game. With less than a minute to play, Montana hit Clark in the back of the end zone for a 6-yard touchdown. The 49ers won 28–27 and advanced to Super Bowl XVI.

HOW MANY FIELD GOALS DID KICKER ROB BIRONAS MAKE TO SET THE SINGLE-GAME NFL RECORD?

Bironas entered the NFL record book when he made eight field goals for the Tennessee Titans on October 21, 2007. Tennessee needed all eight field goals in its 38–36 win over Houston. Five kickers had previously made seven field goals in a game.

CHAPTER 4

HALL OF FAMER

Q **The coldest game in NFL history is known as the Ice Bowl. Who played in that 1967 NFL Championship game?**

A The Dallas Cowboys visited the Green Bay Packers. The temperature in northern Wisconsin was −13 degrees Fahrenheit (−26°C) at kickoff. The wind chill was −48 degrees Fahrenheit (−44°C). The Packers scored a touchdown in the final seconds to win 21–17. It was Green Bay's third straight NFL championship victory.

Q **Which NFL linebacker scored 10 touchdowns on offense during his eight-year career?**

Fans dressed for the cold weather as the Packers faced the Cowboys in the Ice Bowl.

A Even though he was a defensive player, Mike Vrabel caught 10 touchdown passes. Eight of those were with the New England Patriots. Coach Bill Belichick liked to use Vrabel as a tight end when the Patriots got close to the end zone. Sometimes he would block. Sometimes he would catch passes. Vrabel is the only defensive player with two touchdown catches in one game.

Q When was the last time an NFL game finished in a 0–0 tie?

A The last scoreless NFL game was on November 7, 1943. The Giants and the Lions were the last two teams to go an entire game without scoring. The Steelers and the Dolphins almost played four quarters without scoring in 2007. But Pittsburgh won on a 24-yard field goal by Jeff Reed with 17 seconds left in the game.

Q In what year was the first person paid to play football?

A William "Pudge" Heffelfinger became the first professional football player in 1892. The Allegheny

Athletic Association paid him $500 to play in a game. He recovered a fumble for a touchdown in that game.

Q How many total footballs are prepared for use during the Super Bowl?

A Officials get 120 footballs ready before the Super Bowl. That includes 12 special balls for kickers. Wilson is the company that makes footballs for the NFL. Super Bowl footballs are delivered to teams within a day of the AFC and NFC Championship Games. Then teams can practice with them as they get ready for the big game.

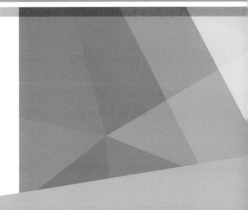

Pudge Heffelfinger is considered the first professional football player.

A Only about 500 sets received the first televised NFL game. NBC aired a game between the Brooklyn Dodgers and the Philadelphia Eagles on October 22, 1939. Television was still relatively new. Not many people had seen a television yet. That has changed, obviously. More than 114 million people watched the Super Bowl in 2015.

Q Where did Arizona and San Francisco play in the first NFL regular-season game outside of the United States?

A The Cardinals and the 49ers met in Mexico for a game in 2005. They played at Azteca Stadium in Mexico City. Arizona beat San Francisco 31–14. The game set a record with 103,467 fans in attendance.

Q What occurred during Super Bowl XLVII in February 2013 to cause a 34-minute delay in the game?

A A power outage at the Superdome delayed the Super Bowl. It happened early in the third quarter with Baltimore leading San Francisco 28–6. After the delay, the 49ers stormed back and made it a game. But Baltimore held on to win 34–31.

Q Los Angeles Rams defensive end Fred Dryer is the only player in NFL history to do this twice in one game. What is it?

A Dryer is the only NFL player ever to record two safeties in one game. On October 21, 1973, Dryer recorded two quarterback sacks in the end zone in the fourth quarter. Dryer's efforts helped the Rams beat the Packers 24–7.

Q Only two players in NFL history have caught 20 or more passes in a game. Who are they?

A Brandon Marshall and Terrell Owens both have had 20-catch games. Owens caught 20 passes with the 49ers in a win over the Bears on December 17, 2000. Marshall broke that record on December 13, 2009. He caught 21 passes for the Broncos in a loss at Indianapolis.

Q Four players are tied with the most Pro Bowl selections in NFL history. How many did they earn?

A The record for the most Pro Bowl selections is 14. Rams defensive tackle Merlin Olsen was the first player to reach that milestone. Offensive lineman Bruce Matthews, tight end Tony Gonzalez, and quarterback Peyton Manning are the other three.

Q Which is the only team to have won multiple Super Bowls without having lost any?

A The Baltimore Ravens are a perfect 2–0 in Super Bowls. The Ravens won their first Super Bowl after the 2000 season. They added a second win 12 years later. Three teams (the Saints, the Jets, and the Buccaneers) are each 1–0 in Super Bowl appearances.

WHICH BILLS PLAYER CAUGHT COWBOYS LINEMAN LEON LETT FROM BEHIND AND PREVENTED A TOUCHDOWN IN SUPER BOWL XXVII?

Lett missed out on a touchdown thanks to the hustle of Don Beebe. The Bills receiver chased down Lett and knocked the ball out of his hand. Lett was celebrating before he had reached the end zone. Despite Lett's blunder, the Cowboys won the Super Bowl 52–17.

TRIVIA QUIZ

1 How many teams are currently in the NFL?

a 30

b 32

c 35

d 40

2 Which expansion team joined the NFL in 2002?

a Seattle Seahawks

b Jacksonville Jaguars

c Houston Texans

d Carolina Panthers

3 Which Hall of Fame quarterback never won a Super Bowl?

a Dan Marino

b John Elway

c Len Dawson

d Johnny Unitas

4 Which city hosted the first regular-season NFL game played outside of North America?

a Berlin

b London

c Tokyo

d Paris

5 **Which of these quarterbacks was not a Number 1 overall draft pick?**

a   Peyton Manning

b   Cam Newton

c   Andrew Luck

d   Aaron Rodgers

6 **Which receiver holds the record for the most catches in a season with 143?**

a   Marvin Harrison

b   Jerry Rice

c   Randy Moss

d   Calvin Johnson

7 **After which former running back is the NFL's Man of the Year Award named?**

a   Jim Brown

b   Barry Sanders

c   Walter Payton

d   Emmitt Smith

8 **To what city did the original Cleveland Browns team move in 1996?**

a   Minneapolis

b   Baltimore

c   Tampa Bay

d   Houston

9 **Which of these NFL players also played professional baseball?**

a   Cris Carter

b   Philip Rivers

c   Maurice Jones-Drew

d   Deion Sanders

10 **In what year was the first indoor football game played?**

a   1902

b   1940

c   1969

d   1980

*Answers on page 47

GLOSSARY

comeback
When a team losing a game rallies to win.

extra point
A kick attempted after a touchdown. It is worth one point.

fullback
One of two types of running backs. Fullbacks are often responsible for blocking for the halfback.

fumble
When a player carrying the ball drops it or has it knocked away from him.

interception
A pass that is caught by a defensive player.

Pro Bowl
The annual all-star game of the NFL.

sack
When the quarterback is tackled by the defense behind the line of scrimmage.

two-point conversion
A play after a touchdown. It is worth two points if the offense makes it into the end zone.

undefeated
When a team does not have a loss in its record.

FOR MORE INFORMATION

Books

Bryant, Howard. *Legends: The Best Players, Games, and Teams in Football*. New York: Philomel Books, 2015.

Gray, Aaron Jonathan. *Football Record Breakers*. Minneapolis, MN: Abdo Publishing, 2015.

Hoblin, Paul. *Andrew Luck*. Minneapolis, MN: Abdo Publishing, 2014.

Websites

To learn more about Sports Trivia, visit **booklinks.abdopublishing.com**. These links are routinely monitored and updated to provide the most current information available.

Answers

1.	b	**6.**	a
2.	c	**7.**	c
3.	a	**8.**	b
4.	b	**9.**	d
5.	d	**10.**	a

INDEX

About the Author

Tyler Mason grew up in Eden Prairie, Minnesota. He earned a journalism degree from the University of Wisconsin-Madison. Mason was in attendance at Qualcomm Stadium in San Diego when Chargers running back LaDainian Tomlinson set the single-season touchdown record in 2006. He currently lives in Hudson, Wisconsin, with his wife.